Pet Guinea Pigs UP CLOSE

by Brynn Baker

Gail Saunders-Smith, PhD, Consulting Editor

CAPSTONE PRESS
a capstone imprint

Pebble Plus is published by Capstone Press,
1710 Roe Crest Drive, North Mankato, Minnesota 56003
www.capstonepub.com

Library of Congress Cataloging-in-Publication Data
Baker, Brynn, author.
Pet Guinea Pigs Up Close / by Brynn Baker.
pages cm.—(Pebble Plus. Pets Up Close)
Summary: "Full-color, zoomed-in photos and simple text describe pet guinea pigs' body parts"—Provided by publisher.
Audience: Ages 5–8.
Audience: K to grade 3.
Includes bibliographical references and index.
ISBN 978-1-4914-2110-9 (library binding)
ISBN 978-1-4914-2324-0 (paperback)
ISBN 978-1-4914-2351-6 (eBook PDF)
1. Guinea pigs as pets—Juvenile literature. 2. Guinea pigs—Anatomy—Juvenile literature. I. Title.
SF459.G9B35 2015
636.935'92—dc23   2014036382

Editorial Credits
Jeni Wittrock, editor; Bobbie Nuytten, designer; Gina Kammer, media researcher; Gene Bentdahl, production specialist

Photo Credits
Alamy: Maximilian Weinzierl, 15; Capstone Studio: Karon Dubke, 1, 7, 9, 11, 13, 17, 19, 21;
Shutterstock: ADA_photo, cover, Marina Jay, 5

Note to Parents and Teachers

The Pets Up Close set supports national science standards related to life science. This book describes and illustrates pet guinea pigs. The images support early readers in understanding the text. The repetition of words and phrases helps early readers learn new words. This book also introduces early readers to subject-specific vocabulary words, which are defined in the Glossary section. Early readers may need assistance to read some words and to use the Table of Contents, Glossary, Read More, Internet Sites, and Index sections of the book.

Printed in the United States of America in Stevens Point, Wisconsin.
092014   008479WZS15

Table of Contents

Purr-fect Piggies

Check out these snuggly guinea pigs! Guinea pigs have body parts that chew, purr, and wheek. Let's take an up-close look at these chatty cavies.

Eyes

Cavies' big eyes see in color,

but they don't see very well.

Guinea pigs have other ways

to know what's around them.

Nose

Sniff sniff! What's that?
Guinea pigs smell predators
before they get too close.
A good sense of smell
helps cavies find food too.

9

Whiskers

Guinea pigs' long whiskers feel everything nearby. In low light, cavies find their way around with their whiskers.

Ears

Guinea pigs' short ears hear well.
They hear sounds humans can't.
Cavies listen for predators, other
pigs, and their favorite people.
Wheek wheek!

Teeth

Did you know cavies purr by chattering their teeth? Piggies have 20 teeth that never stop growing. They chew wood, hay, pellets, and greens.

Legs

Guinea pigs have short little legs. Happy cavies jump for joy, or "popcorn." Careful cavies stay low so predators don't see them.

Feet

Cavy feet have soft pads and sharp claws. Guinea pigs' paw pads let them walk quietly. Claws grip the ground and help piggies groom.

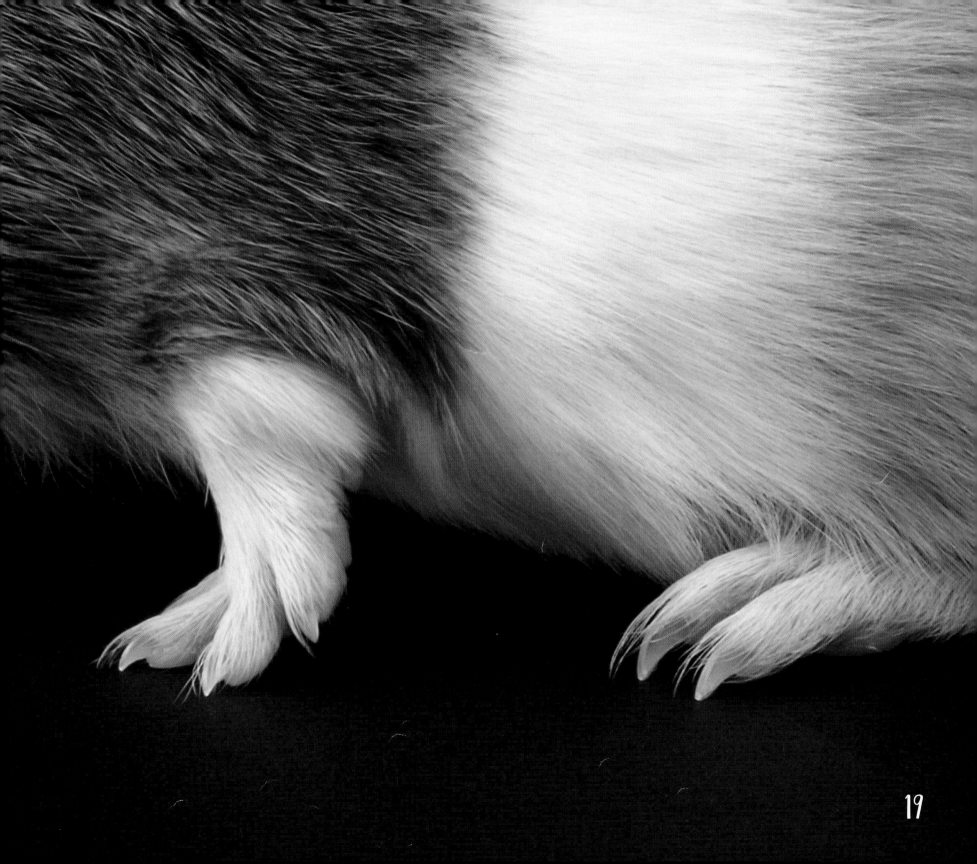

19

Fur

Look at that cute, curly coat! Guinea pig fur has fun colors and patterns. Short fur or long, piggies love to be petted gently. *Chatter, chatter, chatter!*

21

Glossary

cavy—another name for a guinea pig

chatter—to quickly bite teeth together many times; guinea pigs purr by chattering their teeth

coat—an animal's fur

curly—curved or curled

greens—leafy, green vegetables

grip—to hold tight and not slide around

groom—to clean and make an animal look neat

pad—a soft patch of skin underneath an animal's paw

pellet—a piece of dry guinea pig food

popcorn—to jump for joy

predator—an animal that hunts other animals for food

scamper—to run quickly

sense—a way to know what's around you

wheek—a noise an excited guinea pig makes

Read More

Bearce, Stephanie. *Care for a Pet Guinea Pig.* Hockessin, Del.: Mitchell Lane Publishers, 2010.

Ganeri, Anita. *Guinea Pigs.* A Pet's Life. Chicago: Heinemann-Raintree, 2009.

Thomas, Isabel. *Gordon's Guide to Caring for Your Guinea Pigs.* Chicago: Heinemann-Raintree, 2015.

Internet Sites

FactHound offers a safe, fun way to find Internet sites related to this book. All of the sites on FactHound have been researched by our staff.

Here's all you do:

Visit *www.facthound.com*

Type in this code: 9781491421109

Super-cool stuff! Check out projects, games and lots more at **www.capstonekids.com**

Index

Word Count: 208
Grade: 1
Early-Intervention Level: 20

24